To Sell

Influence & Inspire Everyone to Take
Action With This Revolutionary Guide to
Crafting Business Success

Alexandra Masters

To Sell Is Human

Influence & Inspire Everyone to Take Action With This Revolutionary Guide to Crafting Business Success

ISBN-13: **978-0615892115**
ISBN-10: **0615892116**

First Published, 2013
United States of America

Special Thanks to You!

As a special thanks to you, our reader, please accept this FREE gift!

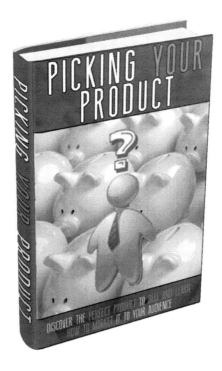

Purchasing this book may have been the first step of your journey to a better life. As a thank you for your purchase, and to help you on this journey, I would like to provide to you a **Guide to Starting a Business From Home Absolutely FREE.**
Download at:
<u>alexandsteven.com/signups/money</u>

TABLE OF CONTENTS

DEDICATION

I dedicate this book to my father.

He is my biggest inspiration to live a happy life. He and my mother make my life worth living.

I hope that one day I can repay them for all they have done for me.

I love you both!
-Alex

We Are All Salesmen

Do you remember not wanting to eat your vegetables, but then convincing your parents to let you eat dessert? Do you remember trying to convince your mom to let you go out to play with your friends while you still had homework, that you would get it done later? You have been a salesman since the time you were young. Maybe you have your own kids now and you try to sell them on things. You try to sell them on why they should or should not go to college. You try to sell them on why they shouldn't drink or smoke. You try to sell your spouse on making dinner.

When you want to sell something, you need to win someone's opinion over on that something. This could be as simple as selling yourself on getting out to mow the lawn or paint the bathroom. See how you even try to sell yourself on things?

When I was in high school I would hit the snooze button about 6 times convincing myself just 5 more minutes won't make me late. I would convince myself that eating one more bite of dessert wouldn't make me fat. We are constantly selling.

Business selling is obviously a little more formal, but the same principles apply.

The Art of Selling & Earning

To master the art of selling, you must master the art of pleasing people. Don't get me wrong, you should be going through life kicking butt, not kissing it. What I mean by pleasing people is adding value to the lives of those who will potentially be customers of yours. If customers are displeased, they will look elsewhere for their needs and wants. You want them to feel as if they owe you something after they have bought something from you.

When you get this kind of response, you develop loyal, repeating customers.

There are many products, informational and physical, available out there that are full of nonsense. Remember, the truth always comes out and you will have a consequence for your actions if you are not honest about what you are selling to people. If you wouldn't buy the product yourself or you wouldn't sell it to a loved one, you really shouldn't be selling that product at all. Ripping people off will keep you broke.

When customers feel you sincerely care about their needs, this builds trust with you. Without trust, you will have a much, much more difficult time selling. It is easy to convince someone you know but it is a thousand times harder to convince a stranger because they do not like you yet or trust you yet. Craig Ballantyne with Early to Rise does a phenomenal job of describing this in his articles. He is a mentor of mine and I have come to trust and like him. So I continue to do what he says because I know he cares about my success and not just the money he could make from me. Now, I don't believe Craig keeps an archive of his previous emails, so just in case, here's the article I am speaking of.

The Truth About Selling

By Craig Ballantyne

Quick. Without using Google, can you guess which personal trainer is worth $200 million and is the 2nd biggest distributor of bison meat in America?

I'll tell you at the end of this article. You'll be shocked. You might also be surprised to know that the fitness experts you see on prime time television are worth only 1% of the $200 million trainer's wealth.

There's a reason why this discrepancy exists. It's not because the $200 million man is a better trainer. Being the most highly skilled trainer, doctor, dentist, plumber, dog trainer or jewelry maker doesn't guarantee you the greatest income. But there is one special skill that brings in the money. And that is the skill of selling.

According to the founder of Early To Rise, Mark Ford, the author of Ready, Fire, Aim, "Selling is the first stage of entrepreneurship... There is a direct relationship between the success of a business at any given time and the percentage of its capital, temporal, and intellectual resources that are devoted to selling."

Learning how to sell is simple.

It all starts with determining what Ford calls, the "Optimal Selling Strategy" for your business.

Where are you going to find your customers?
What product will you sell them first?
How much will you charge for it?
How will you convince them to buy it?

Picking the right product, Ford says, requires the following 5-step process.

1) Find out what products are currently hot in the market.
2) Determine if your product fits that trend.
3) If it does, you are good to go. If not, follow steps #4 and #5.
4) Come up with me-too versions of several hot products.
5) Improve them in a way by adding features or benefits lacking in the originals.

That's a simple system. But I must give you a word of warning. You must not let product creation become a bottleneck in your journey to success. I've met too many potential success stories that have spent months - even years - in the product creation stage. This is unnecessary. If you're building an online business, for example, you should be able to finish your product in no more than four days. Spend one day on research, one day on an outline, and two days recording your content or putting it down in a word document. That's it. Then you must move on to a much more important matter - selling. This is where you need to spend 80% of your time.

Now I know, I know, you "hate selling".

So did I. But in 2003 I recognized that there was one path to the top of the mountain of success. I could continue on the route that led round and round the bottom of the mountain without making any progress, or I could learn to sell and slowly - and eventually rapidly - climb the mountain of success.

Success in sales means overcoming inner, emotional resistance.

"Money," as Dan Kennedy explained, "is attracted to the individual operating free of guilt or shame. People with inferiority feelings about their information, expertise, or business activities are at a profound disadvantage. They subliminally communicate their guilt to others and unconsciously sabotage themselves."

Your success is your responsibility - you must open up your mind to money and fortune. Don't sweep over the essentials of selling by spending time on frivolous matters like Twittering or ordering new office furniture.

There is nothing wrong with selling your solution to the world because you know it works and you know it changes lives. So why are you so reluctant to sell? (I'll let you answer that one to yourself...be honest!).

Almost everyone turns a sickly shade of green when you give the advice, "Learn to Sell". So let me inject a little political correctness into this article. Replace the word selling with "persuading". You must learn to persuade. (Even though they are the same thing!)

The definition of persuasion:
Cause (someone) to do something through reasoning or argument. Cause (someone) to believe something, esp. after a sustained effort; convince.

That's selling. But in a much more politically correct definition, I suppose.

Listen, even Jesus had to sell. First he sold (sorry, "persuaded") his disciples on going out and spreading his word. Then he persuaded the thousands of people that would attend his sermons on the mount. He sold the beggars and the prostitutes on believing in the word of God. And sure, sure, he had the fact that he could perform miracles on his side, but aside from that "minor" advantage, he was still out persuading every day.

The politically incorrect truth is that Christianity didn't grow as big as it is because Jesus and his Apostles dropped off a few Bibles at the Holiday Inns across the Roman Empire. It grew through selling (sorry, PERSUADING) people every day to hear and believe the word of God.

Your business, whether it is online or offline, is not going to grow because you dropped off a couple of slick brochures at a local business or pinned up a sales flyer on the bulletin board of your favorite coffee shop. Even writing a few nice blog posts won't make you money.

You must get over your fear, dislike, and avoidance of selling. You must persuade the world to change.

I'm not exactly sure what is holding you back from making the change, but I can assure you the reason has to do with some sort of internal resistance that you have in your head.

But listen, you must take personal responsibility for everything you do. You must overcome the internal resistance in your life. You must come up with solutions for every obstacle that his holding you back. You must change your mindset. You cannot have self-doubt.

Overcome the resistance, self-doubt, and struggles you are facing by learning to sell. And don't tell me you are too busy. You need to control your time as much as possible. This all starts with identifying your top priorities, doing only what matters, eliminating wasted time (get better at this every day), and accepting personal responsibility for your life.

Stop doing the things that you should not be doing. You can't do it all. Pick what you must do the best and focus on that. And if you are starting a new business, then you must make selling your top priority.

Oh, and about that $200 Million Man?

It's Tony Little. His peers on prime time TV fitness shows are worth only $2 million. Tony is the wealthier trainer because he is the master salesman.

That's the difference the skill of selling can make in your life.

Decide what you want to achieve, and where you want to be, and then take massive action towards getting there. Start with the coaching. Fix your mindset. And then learn how to sell - and make sure that not a day goes by where you aren't SELLING and persuading.

It worked for Tony, it worked for Jesus, and it will work for you.
-Craig Ballantyne, Editor of EarlytoRise.com

Well whaddya think? Craig's a pretty cool guy no? He really helps to motivate people every day to get their lives on track. You can **subscribe to his email for free** at **earlytorise.com** and get a daily dose of quality information that has helped him change the lives of thousands of people.

Making Yourself Stand Out

Maybe you already have a product you are promoting or developing and you want to get it out there, but there is a ton of competition and other products available like yours. How do you get yours to win over customers? Ask yourself this: What makes your product special that a customer should buy yours over others? If you don't know the answer, then how do you expect a stranger to know why he should buy yours? What do you have to offer that makes you unique from the crowd? What makes customers want to keep coming back to you? Ask yourself these questions.

I think it is safe to say we all know we have to walk before we run. When you are in the business of selling, you must be good at it in order to make a living from it. Many people are afraid of selling simply because they don't know how to do it right. People think salespeople are annoying, and they certainly can be. This is where you have the opportunity to stand out from the crowd of other people selling.

If you can get your customer to sell to him or herself on something, you really don't have much work to do besides providing what you have promised. The hardest part of selling is winning over customers- I think we can all agree on this. You need to get down to the core of what your customer wants, find out what their problem is and solve that problem. People are always willing to pay to have problems fixed for them. Let's say you have been selling for years. How do you picture yourself selling to a complete stranger? Do you listen to what the person has to say or are your eyes set on the money before you even catch your potential client's name? You know what sales people are like and you can tell when all they care about is your money. Nobody wants to be that salesperson; nobody wants to buy from that salesperson.

When I am dealing with a business that has poor customer service, I don't care how good their product is. I don't want to deal with them because I don't feel as if they care about me. You have one chance to make a first impression, and if you immediately approach someone with something you want to sell and can't take the time to find out the customer's needs before you bombard them with information that may not even apply to them, you will have lessened your chances of this person buying anything from you. I know I don't like when this happens to me, and I am sure you don't either.

3 Helpful Tips

1. People like to hear their name: When you meet a potential client, find out his or her name and use it throughout the time you are talking with them. It regrabs their attention and you will stand out because so many people don't do this. Your customer is a person with a name to you, not a number.

2. Let your customers talk. Ask them questions so they feel as if you are concerned and really want to get to the bottom of their issues so you can help them with what you have to offer. Again, when you are loyal to your customers, they will be loyal to you.

3. Get their KLT. Before you sell anything, in the words of Craig Ballantyne, get your customer's KLT; they must KNOW you, LIKE you, and TRUST you.

Successful Minds

Successful people have the ability to break out of their comfort zones. They have developed good habits that they practice daily, even if it nobody else is doing so. You see, when you follow the crowd, you end up exactly where the majority of people are in life, which is broke and unhappy. You can develop the habits of successful minds, or you can continue to follow the path you are on. It all really depends on how much change you are looking for in your life. If you stay on the path you are on, then you can expect to be in the same position you are next year and the year after that.

Successful people care about themselves and their customers. There are many rumors about the "rich," such as that they cheated their way to the top or they got lucky somehow. That could be true, but if you plan on getting wealthy this way, I wish you the best of luck because you are going to need it. The truth always comes out, and if you cannot make money in an honest way, eventually you will lose it. Those who do not work for their money are not deserving of it and do not appreciate it. There are jerks out there who are rich and there are jerks who are poor. It really won't help you get any wealthier if you are too caught up in how someone else is making money. Instead, learn from someone who is where you want to be and be 100% teachable. When you become teachable, you become unstoppable.

The more coachable and teachable you are, the farther you will get. That is a fact.

We don't always see what goes on behind the scenes in lives of successful people. The late nights, the stress, the missing out on fun, the dedication, the research, the hard work, these are things that have gotten someone successful where he or she is.

Successful people are able to recognize what they are doing wrong, to fix it and learn from their mistake. They don't let the comfort zone control their life, because opportunity tends to be far outside of it. This is a common thing that gets people stuck, and it can truly be the reason you are where you are. Think of where you would be if you were never afraid to try something new or were not afraid of what failure was like? Failure can take you to new levels in life. It is something to be thankful for because it is part of the learning process.

It Shouldn't Take a Crisis

Are you in a crisis right now? Are you able to put food on the table for your family? Are you laid off from your job? Are you at a breaking point where you just don't know what to do, but you know you need to make a change?

I hope you are not at that point, because it shouldn't take a crisis for you to start taking control over your life. You must be prepared, because only you are in control of what happens to you. Unfortunately, for some people it does take a crisis to realize they need to make a change in their life. This can be with any area of your life, not just finances. How many people wait for a health crisis before taking control of their health? Too many.

Do you really want to wait until you have an illness or even cancer before you start eating better? Do you really want to wait until you are broke before you take the action to make money? No one wants this, yet it happens to so many people. We get so used to a "certain" way of living that we miss what the real opportunities are that are passing us by.

Golden Rule of Habit Change

The number one way to break a habit is to replace it with a new one. Habits are something that our bodies do, some even involuntarily. We all have good habits and we all have bad habits. But the damaging habits need to be recognized and eliminated from your life so that you can progress.

Maybe you like to sleep in late. This I would consider a bad habit. Sleeping in causes you to be unmotivated for the rest of your day and your eating patterns are affected. Maybe you are staying up too late which prevents you from having a proper sleeping pattern and robbing your body of the overnight healing process. Do you see how one bad habit can have a chain of effects? This is what can be known as a habit "loop."

There can be many disadvantages to sleeping in, yet so many people do this for the gratification of not having to wake up early. So, why do so many people have trouble breaking a habit when the bad far outweighs the good? It is because people have trained themselves to be this way and have made it a normal thing in their life. It is up to you to decide how you want to live and when you want to start living the way you have always wanted. Bad habits tend to lead to more bad habits, just like good habits lead to more good habits. What is your loop?

When I first wanted to start eating healthier, I had to come to terms with the fact that I can either keep snacking and begin to develop bad results, or I can take the time now to eat healthier and enjoy delayed gratification. The reward from that is so much more valuable than instant gratification. I got my mindset right before I even started my new lifestyle, and it made it that much easier to stick with the new habit. Eating better helped me to have more energy and to feel better about myself, to boost my confidence and my work ethic. It is amazing how changing one thing can lead to a chain of additional progresses. The same works for money.

When you break your bad habit of spending every dollar you bring in, your bank account starts growing, you have less stress, and you are more likely to invest your money into good things. That will make your money grow instead of going into someone else's bank account.

These are some general examples, but they are very, very real when you become dedicated to changing your life.

If you want to break a habit you know you have, you have to be 100% dedicated to changing it. You cannot say, "I want to lose weight, but I am not that fat so I'll start eating better later". You will continue to be in the exact same shape you are in, and you will have no one to blame but yourself. You are the one in charge of your decisions.

The Craving Brain

Why is it that when we know it is wrong to do something, it can be easier than doing what is right? Have you ever felt so fed up with how you looked that you decided to go on a diet and then 3 days in you break and eat a big dessert? Then you get mad at yourself and instead of learning from your mistake you keep getting yourself into the same vicious cycle?

Our brain craves instant gratification until we train it to think like most people cannot. This skill is so valuable to have. We see something we like on television so we decide we need it now and then complain about paying the bill at the end of the month. "Where did all the money go?" Seems crazy, and so many people are guilty of this. We get so caught up living in the moment that we don't see how it can affect our future. We can't change the past, we can only change the way we grow from it right now, and how we will grow in the future. You can change it right now.

There really is no better time to start, actually.

Society cannot be to blame for your behavior and the position you are in. Some of us choose to follow what everyone else in our society is doing, though, because we don't know what to do. It is our instinct to follow the group because that is where the comfort zone is. We are comfortable making decisions everyone else is making because, "if they're doing it, so should I." Imagine if you started following a group of successful-minded people. Where would you be then? Your norm would be completely different than what it is now. Creating a network of like-minded people you can learn from that are in the position you'd like to be will put you on the right path. You still have to be willing to do the work and to learn to think like a successful person and implement it into your life.

Why Things Catch On & Become Popular

When millions of people are doing something, it tends to make people think that that is what they should be doing also. For example, American Idol was a very popular T.V show to watch for entertainment. Millions of people were watching, and the more that watched the more the word got out and the more popular it became. I personally knew people who did not even like the show, but watched it just because it was the thing to do on that night. People have a hard time making decisions for themselves because they are busy following what other people are doing.

Take a look at where you are. Are you broke like your friends? Did you go into debt going to college to get a degree that you can't use? Did you start drinking in high school because it was cool? Are you drinking every weekend because it is the thing to do now? How are you spending your time and why are you spending it that way? I can almost guarantee that if everyone told you not to go to college you would have been more inclined not to go- and to find an alternative way to make money. I bet you would probably even like what you are doing more.

College is one of the best examples I can think of when it comes to following society. We get out of high school and we don't know what to do with ourselves. After years of the concept that those who don't go to college will be losers is drilled into our heads, it is hard to choose not to go to school. We are so concerned about society and what everyone else is doing we forget about what really makes us happy and how we want to live. As humans, it is our desire to feel special and important. Ironically people think that doing what everyone else is doing is "important." The truth is, when you do what you love to do and you are successful at it and you overcome challenges to get where you want to be, that is when you will feel special and important. That is when you stand out from the crowd and everyone else wants what you have, but will be too afraid to go get it.

80% of the population is in debt. Do you really want to follow the crowd?

When We Care, We Share

When you like something, or you find something really cool, don't you want to tell other people about it? When something is important to us, we like to share it with other people. This is important with business. Don't you want a product that people care so much about they share it with other people? When you solve a problem for someone and add value to their life, they will care about what you have to offer to them whether it is informational products, or a physical product. People want to better their lives and they are willing to pay for it.

I hope that when you are done reading this book, you want to share it with your friends or family members who are in need of help. I am passionate about what I write and I care about what you get out of what I write. I chose to write this book because I have learned these skills that I know will work and wanted to share them. It would be selfish of me not to.

When you are liked and trusted with your customers, you will succeed. They will choose you or they will go somewhere else to meet their needs. It is important to make them feel special and important just as you would like to feel or they will find someone else who will.

Recognizing Potential

There are quite a few tips and tricks on how to sell your products coming up in the following chapters, but right now, let's touch on a topic I mentioned in the previous ones. You can't sell just any product. Customers are a lot smarter than most businesses give them credit for. They are not just "money cattle" that need to be herded into the next big thing for a thorough milking. No, customers can sense sincerity. If you do not believe you are selling a product that can genuinely enhance the lives of those you are selling it to, not only should you not be selling it, but your customers will know sense your lack of sincerity and they will not buy from you.

This chapter is not about how to fake sincerity in order to trick customers into buying things from you. If you've ever read any of my other books, you can attest to one of my mottos, "If you're not honest, you're not in business." This chapter is about recognizing the potential in good ideas and products and utilizing the positivity that product can cause in others' lives to leverage success.

Here's what I mean. A buddy of mine we'll call Chaz makes a pretty decent living coaching others through getting into product categories to sell their items on Amazon.com. Chaz knows that these people may not ever figure out how to get into these categories without his help, and because of this, he knows that he is pushing the best product he can. When his customers are finished with his coaching program, they will have access to a wealth of new sales opportunities on Amazon that they would never have been able to access without him. And when Chaz talks to his customers, they know this. They can sense Chaz's sincerity and confidence in his product because, as I said earlier, Chaz KNOWS there is nothing better than what he has to offer.

Finding the Diamond in the Rough

We all have a million dollar idea within us. For Bill Gates, it was Microsoft, for Steve Jobs it was Apple, and for Chaz it is his Amazon coaching. Is the product you have a millionaire idea? It's okay if it is not, Bill Gates and Steve Jobs didn't wake up as millionaires. In fact, there was a MASSIVE struggle to the top for both of them. They didn't start their businesses with Xbox and the iPod series in their heads. These ideas branched off of smaller ones, as their companies grew. So what do you bring to the table that will help the lives of those around you? It doesn't have to be revolutionary, but you can bring something to the table that will better the lives of those you sell it to, whether it makes things easier, faster, better, stronger, as long as you sincerely believe you're adding value to the world it WILL sell.

Trust the Process

This book is a compilation of the business knowledge and practices proven and established by entrepreneurs around the world. If you haven't found success in your desired field yet or if you are looking to get ahead, you need to take these words to heart.

No one is able to make you a success but you.

Recipe for Success

If your product is going to sell well, it is up to you to create it and market it to the public in a way that has been proven successful countless times, over and over, by worldwide sellers. There is a very special recipe that one must be sure to follow closely if a product is to be sold with the highest conversions possible. The ingredients are as follows: Honesty, Integrity, Simplicity, the Unexpected, Concrete Credibility, and Emotion. All of these ingredients must be wrapped up in a story that your customer can relate to so that the process goes smoothly. How do we combine these ingredients together to make the perfect "Product Pitch Soufflé?

Honesty & Integrity

This is the most important piece of the puzzle. If I've said it once, I've said it a hundred times, "If you're not honest, you're not in business." The key to selling is not to snag a one-time sale. It is to gather a following of loyal, dedicated, sometimes fanatic, customers that will buy what you put in front of them. You do this by earning trust with honesty and integrity. You may be able to sell one product, maybe even two, but your revenue stream will quickly dry up, and you will pay dearly for it if honesty and integrity are not at the core. When your customers find out your true colors and take their business elsewhere, it won't be pleasant.

Simplicity

Your product should be simple to understand or use. Understanding how your product works is not as important as its ease of use, but a brief understanding will help your customers see the value in your product. If they see how your product simplifies a normally complex, or difficult to tackle issue, you're that much closer to a sale. You want your product to be accessible; the more people that can use it easily, the more potential customers you have. Simplicity is a must-have ingredient as people want their life to be simplified with what you have to offer, not made more complex.

Unexpected

Your product pitch needs to include something unexpected, something your potential customer never saw coming. This can range from a free gift, useful advice, another product, or a discount on future purchases. Be sure your unexpected bonus adds SERIOUS value to your product. There is nothing worse than buying a kid's book about a turtle and finding a recipe for turtle soup is being pushed as a free bonus. Your bonus can make your product just as much as it can break it. Chances are, had I seen the turtle soup recipe offer in the book description, I probably would have steered clear. To reiterate, your unexpected bonus for your product should be VALUABLE. Make your customer want not just your product, but the great things it is surrounded by as well!

Concrete Credibility

Let's face it, if you want your product to sell it has to have worked for or benefited someone first. Your sales pitch, sales copy, and/or sales page needs to include some form of scientific data or customer testimonials that shows your prospective buyers that your product is the best of the best. Use a chart of data you've gathered to accentuate your results. Ask one of your previous, happy customers to create a video testimonial, where they showcase the product and talk about how it has affected them. Don't stop at one testimonial, either. As you help more and more people, be sure to update your testimonials page with more and more praise. If someone is going to buy what you have to offer, they need CONCRETE evidence that PROVES that not only will your product work, but it has the best value and does its job better than anyone else's. Don't just say you're the best, PROVE IT!

Emotion

Humans are social creatures and as social creatures we relate to the emotions of others very well. You need to use your sales copy to tap into the emotions of your prospective customers. Which emotion do you choose? Perhaps it is the frustration associated with how difficult something is to accomplish without your product. Maybe you decide to focus on how happy they will be once they have purchased your product.

Don't go crazy though, tap into just one or two emotions and use them to connect with your customer. Relating to your customer builds trust. It helps them see you as more of a friend than a salesman, which is exactly what you want. Think about it, if a stranger comes up to you and tells you to go to store A because their products are better than store B, you might consider it, but you won't act on it. If a stranger sees you're trying to decide between the two stores, introduces himself, and explains to you how he used to shop at store A but due to the frustration from lack of customer service he chose store B, you're much more likely to go to store B instead.

Tell a Story

Customers relate to nothing more than a well-told story. A story helps activate a customer's imagination. It lets them see you as a person who was stuck in a similar situation, and how you came up with the ultimate solution. By telling a story, you'll gain the precious resource that we spoke of earlier, KLT. By telling a story, your customers will get to know you, they will begin to like you, and most importantly, they will begin to trust you. Nothing says sales like trust in a product. If your customer believes the story you tell them, and they relate to you, that trust will not only get them to buy this product, but they will follow you, and convert into long term, returning customers.

So what's this chapter about? It's about honesty. It's about integrity. It's about utilizing simplicity, the unexpected, credibility, emotions, and telling a story to sell your product to not only as many people as possible, but to make sure that those are the happiest customers you've ever had. Take these tips to heart.

These ingredients are crucial in order to have a successful product. If you are missing any of these tips, chances are you're not going to get the maximum sales.

Speaking of ways to boost sales, advertising is a great way to get this magic recipe in front of as many people as possible. But how do you advertise when you don't have the money that the big successful corporations do? What can you do to get the word out?

How to Advertise When You're Broke

If you're selling a product and you're looking for success doing it, chances are you're going to have to get the word out.

Sure, telling a few friends and family may get the ball rolling a bit, but if you're looking to get your product in front of a larger audience you're going to need to advertise a bit.

Here's a list of budget-friendly tips for advertising your product, business, or service.

1. #SocialMedia

Let's talk about the most obvious way first. Everyone has access to social media. The easiest way to get word out for your product is to build a following through social media. If you've got a Facebook page, every "like" is a direct line to your customers and they will hear everything you've got to say. Twitter is very similar. In 140 characters or less you can send out information to any and all of your followers. You probably already know this. The key to social media though is sharing with a purpose.

You may never get the tens of thousands of followers that celebrities can, but you can compete by improving the quality of what you share. You gain followers and likes on Facebook, Twitter, and YouTube by providing value. A big tip is to share often and spontaneously. Social media is a great avenue to gain the beloved KLT that we've spoken of because the more you share, the more your customers will get to know you. Did you just read an article that gave you a great idea for your product? Is it relevant to what you represent? Do you think others would enjoy it as well? Tweet it out or post a link on Facebook. The more you share, the more your followers will care.

Here's an idea I've found to be effective: Go online and look for what's called PLR (Private Label Rights) content that you can give away on a Facebook page for all of your fans that "like" or follow you. This can unleash some exposure that goes somewhat viral as your followers share your useful, relevant content with each other. You don't have to pay for the PLR content, and you can give away something else in your arsenal that you've created yourself, as well. Apply that to an email list from services like **Aweber.com** and suddenly, you've got a ton of "likes", followers, AND email addresses to help showcase your products.

2. Build a Website

Believe it or not, building a website is not expensive. You can actually do it yourself for free if you know where to look. Websites like **wix.com** have plenty of drag-and-drop tools that allow you to make changes quickly, easily, and instantly. As long as you don't mind a few ads on your site promoting Wix, you can put up a great looking site, absolutely free. Check out **alexandsteven.com/angels** for a promotional site I put together through Wix for a special event showcasing my books.

It's very simple, and not only that, but Wix makes it very easy to link to your social media networks as well.

3. Simple Promotional Items

Gaining a lead can be as simple as wearing a **custom t-shirt with your logo on it** or **handing out a few hundred business cards** with your information on them at an event. Promotional items can be purchased for dirt cheap on the internet, and I'm sure it wouldn't be difficult to have a couple friends walk around in a t-shirt that promotes your new Wix website, right?

Heck, even carrying a few pens with your website address printed on them may help you in certain situations. Just leave them lying around, someone will wind up checking you out!

4. Forum Browsing

Many people scoff when you tell them to participate in a forum. They think, "Posting on forums is still a thing? That works?" Yes, actually it does. A quick Google search can bring you to forums about gaming, architecture, science, UFO's and everything in between.

If you post some free, quality information on a few of your relevant sites and become a part of the community, your fellow forum browsers will begin to Know, Like, and Trust you. Where there is KLT, there are sales. It is not a difficult task to accomplish.

Don't go around just posting your products to forums though. Really engage with the community, and maybe throw a little "Check out my website for more info" at the bottom of your posts. Chances are, if you're delivering high quality content, you're going to gain some high quality customers. Do yourself a favor though and don't ever engage in negativity on forums. There are more than enough trolls lurking in the shadows on such sites.

5. Blog Contribution

Believe it or not, the majority of blogs aren't written by just one guy. They are a collaboration of posts from many writers, and as such, they usually have a sizeable following. How do you take advantage of this? In one of two ways. You can either shoot an email to their "Contact Us" page, and request to become one of their contributors OR you can simply post a comment.

You'd be surprised at just how many people sift through the comments of blog sites on the net. Don't just post a little, "I love this article so much!" post. You have to add to the conversation. Actually read the article, and contribute some information, along with a "You can find out more about this on my website" link at the bottom as well.

6. Your Own Blog

Speaking of which, why not start your own blog? Turn your website INTO a blog, or add a link to your blog on your website. It's really simple too. Head over to either **Wordpress.com** or **Blogger.com** and start a site in as little as ten minutes! This is important for a multitude of reasons which are actually quite similar to the reasons for having your own website. For one, a blog gives you a base of operations.

You can send anyone and everyone to your blog and they will learn of everything you've ever posted about. They can learn to KLT you at their own pace, and learn of everything you're currently working on and involved in all in one place. What many bloggers find difficult is how to ensure they're not "giving away too much content." There is a simple answer to this question.

All you need to do is make sure you are providing what I like to think of as incomplete content. What this means is that you are not providing a full course that explains anything and everything regarding the subject at hand. Give your readers a taste, and then either "push" a product or an advanced feature they can utilize (like a subscription plan) for the full story. For example, let's say you're running a blog about email lists.

You would want your article to be something along the lines of "The top 5 reasons to build an email list." Then, go ahead and write your blog post. At the end of the post, put your offer out to the customer. "Want to know how you can build a list too? Upgrade to Premier Member Status and learn ALL the ins and outs of list building!"

Blogs also help drive traffic to your site through search engines. Make sure your blog titles and content include your key search terms and you will experience a tidal wave of traffic sweeping over your site after you post it.

7. Make a Post on Craigslist

Craigslist has a massive amount of traffic- traffic you can utilize with a simple classified ad. It's free. It's simple. It's effective. Just paste your sales copy into their posting field, along with any pictures and links you'd need to include, and let Craigslist's traffic do all the work.

All in all, your business will always do well if you make sure you have excellent customer service and you're offering a high quality, genuine product. I'm repeating this over and over again because it is so vitally important: "If you're not honest, you're not in business." Your best new customers are your old customers and by making sure that you're providing the best product or service you possibly can and gaining all that beloved KLT in the process, your business is sure to be a success. Happy customers don't only continue buying from you, but they cause a ripple effect. They tell their friends who become happy customers who tell their friends who become happy customers, and so on and so forth.

By not building a network of valued, loyal customers you're robbing yourself of success. Don't let that happen to you and use the information I've provided. Take some action, and get the word out about your business today!

Find a Mentor

We visited this topic earlier. We all know that reinventing the wheel can be a dreadful thing to do. Trying to be completely unique and dreaming up some idea that no one else on Earth has come up with is not fun!

There is most likely someone out there who is in the same field you want to be in and is successful in that field, whatever it may be. It could be cooking, selling, writing, drawing, playing an instrument, and so on. There are experts in any field. The internet gives us a whole new world of opportunity to contact people easily and to search for our answers. We have the ability to join different mentoring groups with people from 20, 30, 40, or 50 different places to learn from each other. When you create a network of like-minded people, what they do will become your norm. You begin to pick up the good habits they have to offer and it will make every step you take out of your comfort zone a little easier than if you had no one to help show you the way.

If you find someone who is where you want to be in life, and they are willing to show you how they did it, you have a blueprint laid out for you. You must be 100% coachable by that person because the or she is the one who has succeeded. If you are being coached and you think of 100 reasons why not to take the advice they are giving, they would rather not take your money and not have to deal with someone who must not need their help anyway. They'd rather give valuable time and lessons to someone who is willing to take their advice to heart, because they have walked the walked and have done what they are trying to help you to do.

Having a closed mind will always delay you. Have you been reading this and thinking to yourself, "I don't have to do all of that to sell better," or "The way I have been selling has been working out for me so far." Why did you buy this book if you are already at the top of your game? You bought this book to learn something new, so hopefully you'll take action even if it is not what you wanted to hear. Not everything is going to be what you want to do or the easiest thing to do, but the important thing is to do it and to never let failure bring you back. Failure, in my eyes is a step forward. When I fail at something, I know I tried something a million people will never even try to do, and I learn from the bad and turn it into good.

You bought this book as a way to learn and to better yourself and I admire you for that. You are already way ahead the crowd.

It can be a very scary thing to start something completely new in your life, or to even change a habit you have had your entire life. Maybe you already are in sales and you have been selling a certain way for 15 years. You're thinking that you could never take the advice I am giving, or you just wont be good enough at it. Always remember that your thoughts become actions and your actions define who you are. If you tell yourself over and over you can't do something, most likely you will never even try to do it.

Our brains were designed to take information and to learn from that information. We should continue to learn throughout our whole life. The more valuable information you learn, the more you grow. You must be wise about who you are trusting with teaching you when it comes to making a better life for yourself.

If I was going to learn how to start up a business and I had a good friend who had a successful business for 30 years and I also had a friend who was struggling to get by day to day for the past 30 years, which person would I ask for advice? Obviously, I would certainly ask the person who has been successful at what I wanted to do, and maybe even try to recognize what my other friend is doing wrong.

My Story of Finding a Mentor

When I was 18 years old, I applied to an entrepreneurship and liberty camp put on by extremely successful businessmen. The coaches were Simon Black, Craig Ballantyne, Sam Wolanyk and Matt Smith. All of them are self-made multi-millionaires and they hold this camp in Lithuania every year for 50 young adults. They have a 4 day class which they pay for completely, you just have to find your way to Lithuania. I was from the USA, and there were young men and women from about 40 different countries there.

You can bet I was put out of my comfort zone on that flight to the camp. I was an 18-year-old kid that had to face 4 successful men and try to keep up with what they were teaching. It was on of the best decisions of my life to apply. To this day I follow those coaches' advice, and anyone can follow great coaches' advice if they so choose.

I made my application video and I was completely honest about where I was in life and where I wanted to be. Three months later I was on my flight overseas and I got to spend the week with not only like-minded coaches, but like-minded attendees that I still keep in contact with. We fed off each other and learned amazing things from each other. It was great to be with 49 other young adults from around the world sharing thoughts, ideas and learning.

I had begun my first meaningful network. We all have to start somewhere, and there was nothing special about me beside the fact that I think differently than most of the people I know. "When you live a few years of your life like no one will, you can live the rest of your life like no one can."

I Really Do Admire You

I want to first thank you for giving me the opportunity to write for you. There is nothing to hold you back when you open your mind to new ideas. I may sound redundant because I keep making this point, but I want it to be imbedded into your thought process. You can become a selling guru as soon as you start taking action. We all have it in us to sell; we just need the skills. There are people all around the world who implement the same ideas I shared with you in this book. The only one that is holding you back is you. Put this book to use, because I did not write it for it to collect dust on a shelf or to take up a little extra space in your kindle. Be confident in how you work, be honest, humble, giving, hard-working and open-minded, and you will be unstoppable.

Good luck.
-Alexandra Masters

Wait Before You Go!

As a special thanks to you, our reader, please accept this FREE gift!

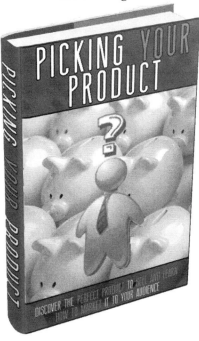

Purchasing this book may have been the first step of your journey to a better life. As a thank you for your purchase, and to help you on this journey, I would like to provide to you a **Guide to Starting a Business From Home Absolutely FREE.**
Download at:
alexandsteven.com/signups/money

Resources

1. Early to Rise Newsletter Signup

http://www.earlytorise.com/authors/cb

2. To Start Your e-mail List

http://www.aweber.com

3. To Build Your First Website (FREE)

http://www.wix.com

4. To See My FREE Wix Site

http://www.alexandsteven.com/angels

5. To Get a Custom T-shirt

http://www.spreadshirt.com/design-your-own-t-shirt-C59

6. Business Card Sites

http://www.businesscardstar.com

http://www.vistaprint.com

7. Start a Blog!

http://www.Blogger.com

http://www.Wordpress.com

8. For More Books by Me, Alexandra Masters

http://www.alexandsteven.com/angels

Search: Alexandra Masters on AMAZON!

ISBN-13: **978-0615892115**
ISBN-10: **0615892116**
(A&S Publishing)

Printed in Great Britain
by Amazon